# Feeling Out

By: Carolyn Fado & Kelly Inviere

Text Copyright © 2019 by Carolyn Fado
POWER Text Copyright © 2019 by Carolyn Fado and Kelly Inviere
Image Copyright © 2019 by Kelly Inviere
Role Away Image Copyright @ 2019 by Jean Wogaman

ISBN: 978-1-62429-256-9

All rights reserved. This book or any portion thereof may not be reproduced or used in any manner whatsoever without the express written permission of the author except for the use of brief quotations in a book review.

Published through Opus Self-Publishing Services
Located at:
Politics and Prose Bookstore
5015 Connecticut Ave. NW
Washington, D.C. 20008
www.politics-prose.com // (202) 364-1919

Feeling Out

## Dedication

I (poet) try—labor in labyrinths lit by love—to write
the maze of emotion you set into motion,

you,
my muse.
Every poem
painted page
plays out
words
lines
letters
feelings out
all ways always
leading me to you

—all I write,
my words can't do you justice when all I wrote is just this. All I
write I can't get right for you.
I try to write
out love
for you.

# Feeling Out

**Denying Words**
Crushed . . . . . . . . . . . . . . . . . . . . . . . . . . . . . . . . . . . . . . . . . 10
To Be A Good Girl . . . . . . . . . . . . . . . . . . . . . . . . . . . . . . . . 12

**My Poetic Diary**
My Poetic Diary . . . . . . . . . . . . . . . . . . . . . . . . . . . . . . . . . 15
Secrets . . . . . . . . . . . . . . . . . . . . . . . . . . . . . . . . . . . . . . . . 16
I Don't Like-Like you . . . . . . . . . . . . . . . . . . . . . . . . . . . . . 17
Don't Deny . . . . . . . . . . . . . . . . . . . . . . . . . . . . . . . . . . . . . 18
I Admire . . . . . . . . . . . . . . . . . . . . . . . . . . . . . . . . . . . . . . . 19
That's A Low Cut Top . . . . . . . . . . . . . . . . . . . . . . . . . . . . . 20
Un-Huggable. Friend? . . . . . . . . . . . . . . . . . . . . . . . . . . . . 21
Signals . . . . . . . . . . . . . . . . . . . . . . . . . . . . . . . . . . . . . . . . 22
Thoughts Of You . . . . . . . . . . . . . . . . . . . . . . . . . . . . . . . . 23
Love Less . . . . . . . . . . . . . . . . . . . . . . . . . . . . . . . . . . . . . 24
Conversation Of The Eyes . . . . . . . . . . . . . . . . . . . . . . . . 25
Should I . . . . . . . . . . . . . . . . . . . . . . . . . . . . . . . . . . . . . . . 26
I Can't Realize. . . . . . . . . . . . . . . . . . . . . . . . . . . . . . . . . . 27
We Lie . . . . . . . . . . . . . . . . . . . . . . . . . . . . . . . . . . . . . . . . 28
Heartbeat . . . . . . . . . . . . . . . . . . . . . . . . . . . . . . . . . . . . . 29
I Used To Keep A Diary, . . . . . . . . . . . . . . . . . . . . . . . . . . 30
Words A Blur, . . . . . . . . . . . . . . . . . . . . . . . . . . . . . . . . . . 31
Who Am I Without My Thoughts? . . . . . . . . . . . . . . . . . . 33
She Could Have . . . . . . . . . . . . . . . . . . . . . . . . . . . . . . . . 34

## Admission To Self
Legend Of The Girl With Mirror Eyes . . . . . . . . . . . . . . . . . . . 38
I Want To Listen . . . . . . . . . . . . . . . . . . . . . . . . . . . . . . . 39
Are You Aware? . . . . . . . . . . . . . . . . . . . . . . . . . . . . . . . 40
Do I Repulse You? . . . . . . . . . . . . . . . . . . . . . . . . . . . . . 41
Do I Dream Of You . . . . . . . . . . . . . . . . . . . . . . . . . . . . . 42
Thy Sonnet, My Love . . . . . . . . . . . . . . . . . . . . . . . . . . . 43
Never-Ending Kiss . . . . . . . . . . . . . . . . . . . . . . . . . . . . . 44
Lavender Love . . . . . . . . . . . . . . . . . . . . . . . . . . . . . . . 45
Cantamos . . . . . . . . . . . . . . . . . . . . . . . . . . . . . . . . . . 46
A Saint Assistance, As Ain't Assistance . . . . . . . . . . . . . . . . . 47
El Unicornio . . . . . . . . . . . . . . . . . . . . . . . . . . . . . . . . . 48
Why Can't You Behave? . . . . . . . . . . . . . . . . . . . . . . . . . 51
Yes, That's What My Smiles Means . . . . . . . . . . . . . . . . . . . 52
Bi . . . . . . . . . . . . . . . . . . . . . . . . . . . . . . . . . . . . . . . 52
Humanity's Exists in Me . . . . . . . . . . . . . . . . . . . . . . . . . 55

## Amusing Truth

| | |
|---|---|
| Amusing Truth | 57 |
| Write For You | 58 |
| Dear Muse, | 59 |
| Drink Sin In | 60 |
| They Tell Me We Kissed. | 63 |
| Singing Spirit | 64-65 |
| When Poetry isn't Sex. | 66-67 |
| Straight/Gay | 69 |
| Do I?. | 70 |
| Today | 71 |
| My Darling, Speak!. | 72 |
| Speak In Kisses. | 73 |
| Genius Brain | 74 |
| Place Alone | 75 |
| I Am A Contrapuntal. Can You Read All Of The Poetry In Me? | 76 |
| Role Away | 77 |
| Stay | 77 |

## Coming To Terms

Coming To Terms . . . . . . . . . . . . . . . . . . . . . . . . . . 79
When The Right Is Always Right—And The Left Is Always Left . . . . . 80
Fatigue-ly Feeling Bliss—this?. . . . . . . . . . . . . . . . . . . 81
Just Another Dose Of Coffee . . . . . . . . . . . . . . . . . . . . 83
How Can I . . . . . . . . . . . . . . . . . . . . . . . . . . . . . 84
Hetero/Homo . . . . . . . . . . . . . . . . . . . . . . . . . . . . 85
When The Rhymes Don't Come . . . . . . . . . . . . . . . . . . . . 86
???? . . . . . . . . . . . . . . . . . . . . . . . . . . . . . . . 87
Female, Framed . . . . . . . . . . . . . . . . . . . . . . . . . . 88
The Toll . . . . . . . . . . . . . . . . . . . . . . . . . . . . . 89
Her: A Hymn . . . . . . . . . . . . . . . . . . . . . . . . . . . . 90
ShhhHE. . . . . . . . . . . . . . . . . . . . . . . . . . . . . 92-93
Shy Girl . . . . . . . . . . . . . . . . . . . . . . . . . . . . . 94
POWER. . . . . . . . . . . . . . . . . . . . . . . . . . . . . . . 96
Inner Piece . . . . . . . . . . . . . . . . . . . . . . . . . . . . 97
Set Your Journey.... . . . . . . . . . . . . . . . . . . . . . . . 99

## About The Artists

About The Authors . . . . . . . . . . . . . . . . . . . . . . . . 101
Artists' Note . . . . . . . . . . . . . . . . . . . . . . . . . . 102

## Denying Words

The her in brother brought her
The miss in mister missed her
Little Miss Gender
Play pretender
Not pretend her.

# Denying Words

## Crushed

"Hey." I wave.
I barely speak, but blush
below you,
meek.

To save myself distress, I don't dare express how I'm obsessed.
I'd best repress, but, nonetheless,
your sexy smile sets my heart to race.

Counting the times you look at
me (1,2,3), I wonder if you
see emotions spark from inside
me while I try to
be still.

Oh, the thrill of imagining what I will.

Why can't I just chill, chill?

Say swallow sweet feelings,
can't show a trace, but
can't break my blush to save my face.
My sad, shy
smile leaves a
trace.

Your sexy smile sets my heart to race.

## To Be A Good Girl

They told me acting as I should
would make me good.

*How could they know?
I don't know,
but they showed such
conviction, as they
spoke with perfect
diction, telling me
how to be.*

I mimicked, willingly,

afraid
that I could one day see
*the villain inside that's
part of me.*

Feeling Out

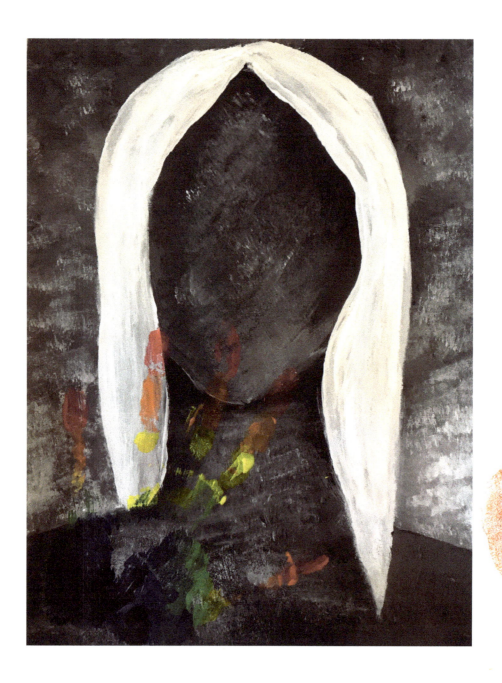

Feeling Out

# My Poetic Diary

It's what all princesses dream of...

a prince
to carry me
away

a $$$$
$$ sexy ride
$$$$

They
call me
C.M. Love

One     Day
I'll change my name
for love

Cary M. Love tries to live a perfect life,
a fairy-tale dream, a king for a queen,
but happiness is not as it may seem.
Overcome by inner-strife, Cary turns
to art to live their life.

Feeling Out

## Secrets

Should I tell you that I think about you—or rather that I want to think about you, but that I can't give myself permission? I'd rather change the topic in my brain than go through the pain of analyzing how I think about you. When I wake up and you're in my thoughts—why? Did I just dream about you? I don't remember my dreams. Is it normal to think about you like this? I won't allow myself to go remiss. I could just want you as a friend.

Dear reader, please don't judge me. And if it's you who's reading, please don't realize this is about you. I don't know what could happen if you were to find out. It's nothing, though I dread and yearn for something. Do I tell you my thoughts—or rather that I try not to think of you a lot? I may say that I forgot that time you sat next to me, our awkward hug greeting. I pretend to forget. Try to not think. I can't remember everything about you, then you'd know. Then I'd know.

## I Don't Like-Like You.

I just like you.

The way you smile at
everyone in the room
and make them feel special makes me want to feel extra special.
I just want to be like you,
to have your charisma, *tu inteligencia*.
I want to spend a day inside your— *mind*—to learn how to be like you.

## Don't Deny.

I am not a lesbian. I've had a crush on a guy,
so why is it that I can't help but stare at
more than your eyes?
I can help it. I try to justify. I just admire
your *manera de ser*.
You inspire.

## I Admire

your smile,
your laugh,
how you can find the humor in everything
while here I am stressing
and repressing.
You help me quit my second guessing,
opening me up with laughter.
Your look is cool but not pretentious,
stylish and low-key,
leaving me feeling free while wishing I could be
as cool as you.

**That's A Low-Cut Top.**

Only guys think that way. It bugs me when they leer
and bring their burly bodies near
for buxom hugs.
And... I start... to wonder...
I'm not gay.

## Un-Huggable. Friend?

Can I hug you?
One hug, takes so much thought,
my emotions overwrought
for each hi and bye. I inch forward,
I stay an inch away.
With them, just any him or her, I'd hug them easy, but—
I'm scared to hug you.
If I dared to hug you,
would the thousand sparks fire
of my can-I-call-it desire?

## Signals

I imagine
our blunder bump of hands
was planned and yet
      unplanned…
      the second I
traced your
lingering fingers
remembered and erased
from my memory.
My cheeks hot, I near forgot
yet only thought of
who we were
      who we weren't
where we were
      where we weren't
as I took in
the look upon your face,
the twinkle in your eyes.
"Do you feel it too?" I wondered,
      fearing hearing, "yes, I do,"
      yearning hearing, "yes, I do."

## Thoughts Of You

Are they true?

## Love Less

Desire unheard, my
emotions feel blurred—
wondering what occurred, dreaming what is,
what never is, what will never be.
I can't see you and me.

## Conversation Of The Eyes

Look into The Words are only my eyes. we may devise lies.

I don't speak when our eyes meet for a heartbeat. Why the heartbeat? I cannot say I feel this way. I dream the conversation of our eyes belies our lack of words, for so it seems.

## Should I

tell you that I can't stop thinking about you?

## I Can't Realize

the real in our eyes. You above,
me below,
let's say it's our
look of lies
that defies
our wise tries of
hoping our desire dies,
and now we
lie.

## We Lie

head to head.

## Heartbeat

Hushing, rushing, energy,
blushing—it's nothing—they will not see
you and me as we
are
*avoiding breathing*—it's nothing—

*hay algo*. It's something.

**I Used To Keep A Diary,**

but now it doesn't feel right. Am I feeling a lie?
If I try, I can deny.  I used to like a guy.
I used to love a guy.  Didn't I?

## Words A Blur,

no thoughts occur. If there were
I'd I've stopped them for sure
because of
her,
thoughts of her.
Not of her. I got to
not get caught. Think thoughts as I was taught. Lots, sought,
wrought. I rot, acting as I ought.
Ramble rot, for naught, forgot.

## Who Am I Without My Thoughts?

Descartes wrote "I think, therefore I am."
When I don't think, then,
who am I?
Let's say I'm nobody, who are you?
When I don't think, then,
can I know you?
You taught me the art of losing all my thoughts—
pretend I haven't got a lot—
I forgot as I have sought.
I hear that song, I sing along,
even when I feel it's wrong.

**She Could Have**

She could have
anyone she wanted—
and this—*this*—is *her*
bliss?
Imagine their kisses—
he hisses,
"Miss,
what did I miss?"

Feeling Out

# Admission to Self

Feeling Out    37

## Legend Of The Girl With Mirror Eyes

Mirror eyes,
sweet as a dove,
reflect the love you
princes dream of.

There was a young lady
with mirror eyes.
That girl was
me. I'd hidden all
I'd ever be.

## I Want To Listen

I want to listen to you
as two people listen best,
forgetting what's repressed.
If you want me, come
on back my way.
If you don't want me, then I'll go
away.

Let's listen soul-to-soul,
hearing, feeling, seeing, sensing,
speaking, touching whole.

## Are You Aware?

In my dreams, we had a child.
I hardly know you, so it's wild.
Unrequited love is creepy.
You're in my thoughts
as I imagine,
doing things you might not fathom.

But, oh, the
comfort you bring!
My heart flies and sings.

## Do I Repulse You?

If I could recreate myself
into the splendor of someone else,
would you love me?
If I were famous,
if I were male,
if I were quick-witted,
if I were wealthy?

## Do I Dream Of You?

or of...
only how you seem?
Are you
how I see you to be,
that is, are you perfect
for me?
The you
who has won my heart,
the you whom I imagine,
consumes me
with a passion.

## Thy Sonnet, My Love

For my love sonnet to be true to thee,
'Twill need to be a play, a song, a dance,
Awakening the earth, the sky, the sea
And capturing the reader in a trance.

As if my sonnet compares to thee! No,
Not to thy sweet complexity, thy face,
Thy power to change time, both fast and slow,
Nor to the magic sparks of thine embrace.

**F**or thee, I copy the great bard, his style,
**A**s if my words could even that allow,
**I** hope thou find'st my words to be worthwhile.
**L**ove, you need more—not this informal *thou*:
      You are the queen of my poor beating heart.
      Quite simply, my queen, my love, you are *art*.

## Never-Ending Kiss

We yearn for this,
*so*
kiss me fast and
*long*.
Let's hold the feeling
we
belong.

## Lavender Love

Call me a **shrinking** violet

They dress up in rainbows to celebrate lavender love.
Blue is my warmest color.
I'm green with envy for their pride,
for the cis gay guys, without a question,
even straight ones there who march beside.
I stand behind the curtains, I'm inside.
How could I deny these golden locks
their prince
when, once upon a time, I dated a prince?
Oh, the shock that I...
that I'd ... defy these golden locks.
I'm locked, but
oranges are not the only fruit,
so stamp a scarlet letter
across my chest,
on my own heart beating breast.

I am not a shrinking **violet**
for our lavender love.

Feeling Out

## Cantamos

Do not trust alone—your sight—
it takes many to get it right.

In the future, let my words be wrong—
you will have added to my song,
it is our song,
we both belong,
we all belong—
singing alone,
it comes
out
wrong.

## A Saint Assistance As Ain't Assistance

Saint Assistance
we're allies
together,
with one
another.

Saint Ass I Stance
we're all lies
to get her,
with one,
a not her.

## El Unicornio

I've learned I don't exist.

Unicorns
exist in legends only,
they say.
My voice is hoarse,
I don't exist,
you will not see me in the daylight,
at least not with such
poetry as this,
I can't write.

They all tell me to
hoarse my voice
without a choice,
except for you.

Should I live my life a horse,
led by a jockey on life's course
so I can win the race,
cut to the chase:
first, second, third base,
run back to home,
straight-laced?

As I child I would play
pretend.
I knew I had a horn

when I was born,
but then my mommy
warned me that the world will
capture unicorns.

To you, I'll
say I can't make magic,
pretend I don't have magic.
To be uniform, I'll hide my horn,
afraid that it will bring me scorn.

My voice is
more than just a simple
neigh, nay—
for I have many things to say,
Carolyn my singing way.

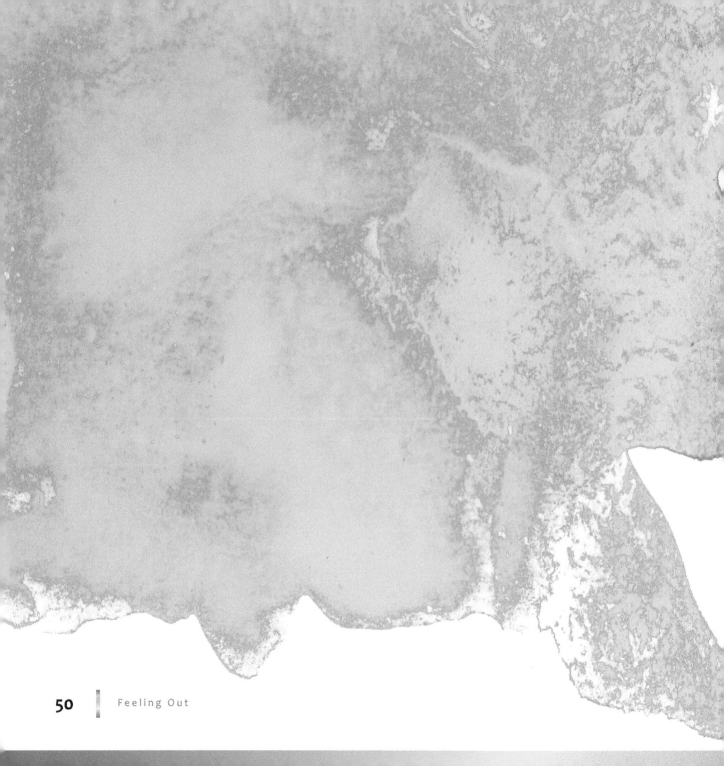

## Why Can't You Behave?

The
world *mis*sed us, we're
out. Let us *be*, let
us exist. Let us *have* our
dreams.

### Yes, That's What My Smile Means.

For him, I too have thoughts obscene—
but, oh, he's seen me with a queen.

### Bi

They see me with a guy,
they think that it must be my try
to deny
my beating heart.

Feeling Out

## Humanity Exists in Me

Let me be

somewhere that isn't
fe/male
s/he
wo/man,
somewhere unique,

somewhere my soul
can freely speak.

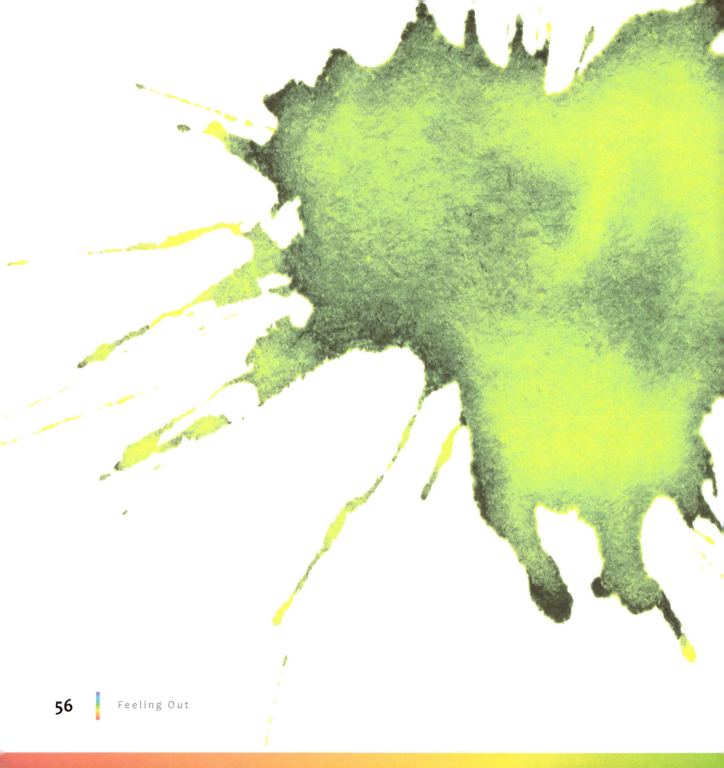

# Amusing Truth

My Love, if you could count the times I've lied, to myself or someone else, you'd doubt my **pride**. How can I know when to confide or when it's safer to hide my truth insid**e**? Through the years, I've tried to live a picture-perfect dream- *that girl*'s dream, success as it may seem, a king, for a queen, Like my inner **e**xistence is an act of defiance, I've developed a reliance on playing a role. In **l**ieu of being my whole, I've lived two me's inner self, outer someone else-*that girl* designed to please; to keep them all at ease, I've tr**i**ed to live without your kisses, your love, tried **n**ot even to dream of finding love-*that* **g**irl has a rich, male lover, and damn the lady lover **I am!** But, then, there's you. I gaze int**o** your eyes, alive. I realize myself in love with yo**u**. I want to be me, myself. **T**rue.

Feeling Out

## Write For You

I wrote one poem about you.
Actually, I wrote you two
because it's you.
Actually, I wrote you three,
you inspire me poetically.

Actually, I wrote you four—
and then five more.
You make me feel alive.

I'll write you nine
plus ten
and more again
and again.

**Dear Muse,**

my words can't do you justice,
when all I wrote is just this.

## Drink Sin In

I drink
alcohol
to give me the wherewithal
so I can fall
and make a fool of myself
while I still stay cool
for everyone else.

They say it's the alcohol
that makes me fall. But,
I drink for
each little sip
that lets me trip.

I have already fallen.

It's not the alcohol
that makes me fall
in love with you.

Is such inebriation
necessary to seize
what our souls' seek?
Because
in normal life,

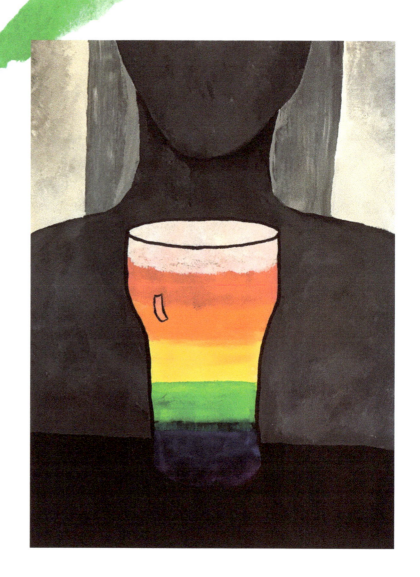

we stand too meek…

Is such inebriation
necessary to
forget how being gay is bleak,
to forget that I'm a freak?

We kiss at the party—
*two drunk women*—
we kiss in the daylight—
two lesbians.

The night is over.
Overcome by desperation,
I wake to my
sobering frustration/elation
that you balance my equation

♀ + ? = ♥
♀ + ♀ = ♥
me + you = ♥

## They Tell Me We Kissed.

I'm
sobering up to
live it out.
Erase my doubt.
I'm coming out.

## Singing Spirit

*Close your eyes and you can hear it.*

    my heart beat skips
    in harmony, yearning for the symphony
    of our kiss, every beat
      skip
    beat
      skip
    beat
    dancing, skipping
    in reply to the melodic twinkle of
    your eye, every beat
      skip
    beat
      skip
    beat
    my try to meet that melodic twinkle of
    your eye, every beat
      skip
    beat
      skip
    beat
    my chance to entice you to dance
    as you sashay in circles
    my way, every beat
      skip
    beat

  skip
beat
my try to be, to breathe your harmony
as you circle around me,
so close you gaze into my eyes,
so close your arms around me,
so close you feel my chest rise, you
close your eyes,
so close our chests rise and
fall together, as my beat
  skip
beat
  skip
beet meets your
  skip
beat
  skip
beat, together
beat. beat. beat.

## When Poetry Isn't Sex

You love the way I use my tongue
in four languages—
but never in the one I'd find most fun.

You love just this
poetic kiss
and ask for it again.

I late-night-speak
in metaphor,
you'd never care
to ask for more.

Remember when you asked before?

We found
our human touch a tragedy,
reminding us we cannot be
together in this way—to you, it does
not feel okay. To me, I will not let it
feel okay.

But, oh, how I desire you. You say
the stroke of my pen opens your hips,
when my words come from another's lips.
My hand entreats your heart to sing,
my hand upon the page.

I'll never...
my hand can never dance on...

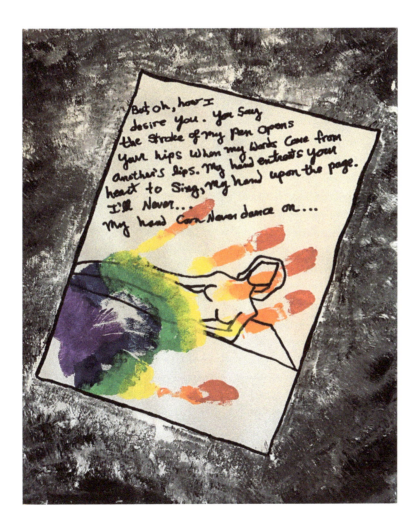

## Straight/Gay

It's you I love,
so to be true to you
I'll bid my fantasies to just be through,
I'll be your truest friend
until the end.
Is that too much for me
to comprehend?
Cupid Ain't Shit

### Do I?

Do I?

dare to share
how you inspire
sparks
fireworks
of my
desire?

This life is not forever.
I'd rather walk together,
in friendship
or however.

## Today

*Just seeing you
can make my day.
I feel your gaze,
I'll be okay.*

## My Darling, Speak!

Lack of language makes love weak.
Even when you feel your words are bleak, don't tweak them.
Speak them.

Speak in many ways,
show me over many days.

## Speak In Kisses

Please express
what speaking syllables
solomente
leads us to repress.

## Genius Brain

*Am I going insane?*
*I can no longer contain*
*myself. I can't refrain.*

black　or white,
　　　　　　am I
　are we
　　gay　　or　　straight
　　　　　　are you
　are we
happy　　or　　sad
smart　　or　　stupid
　ugly　　or　　beautiful
healthy　　or　　sick
　dead　　or　　alive
honesty　or　　lies
　truth　　or　　fiction
right　　or　　wrong
　short　　or　　tall
nothing　　or　　all
　rise　　　or　　fall
you　　　or　　me
　can I be　　apart
　　　and free
　　　my victory
　　　your loss
　　　by and by
follow　　or　　defy
　　fit the binary
　　　wary
I am　　or　　I ain't
　I shall　or　I shain't.
　　evil　or　saint

　without a trace
the emotions you face

**Place Alone**

## I Am A Contrapuntal. Can You Read All Of The Poetry In Me?

| | |
|---|---|
| I am | of course |
| normal, but | I am also different |
| they label me by what I'm not, | call me |
| non-white | non-black |
| not cis | not trans |
| not straight | not gay |
| not affluent | not poor |
| not healthy | not sickly |
| | |
| accept me, | remember I'm different, |
| when I'm not their "same," | even when I fit their sameness, |
| let me | undo the norm and |
| live | free! |

## Role Away

I play my part
I take my/self a/part.

art by J Wogaman

## Stay

They tell me I have nowhere to go,
but I'm now *here*, I know.

# Coming To Terms

*Before I speak
I feel it out,
the situation,
gaging if what I say
will be okay.*

## When The Right Is Always Right—And The Left Is Always Left

and you're left-handed
because to you,
the left is
right.
It just feels right,
but they say it isn't right.

You write to say
you have a right to use
your left to write and
not be left behind.

Write out the beauty
of your mind.
            Left out the beauty of your mind.

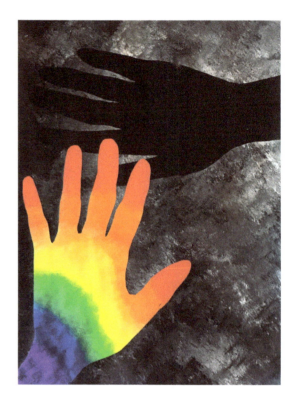

## Fatigue-ly Feeling Bliss—this?

Let me be tired,
'til I no longer care,
'til I am blissfully unaware.

In my busyness,
I aim for the prize,
to be the envy of your eyes,

pushing my soul through a disguise—
not quite my whole
but a perfect lie—
as I deny.

I can try to be the best.
It'll help me to forget the rest,
as I confess
inside my mind
that I'm leaving my soul
behind.

Perhaps you'll find
my soul up high
and 'll get to know
my spirit by and by,
through all my lies.

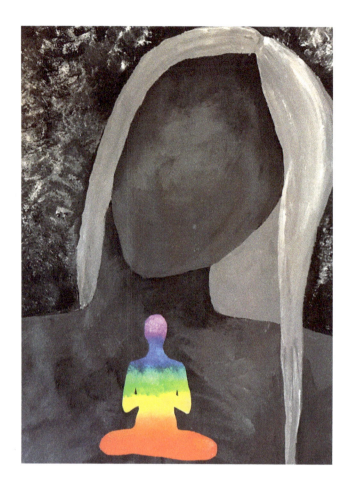

Am I alive
      to free my spirit, or
           am I alive to be a
              worker bee
              in a hive,
        as I strive for it—
      for what they
              say a soul
          should strive?

## Just Another Dose Of Coffee

Say, we will breathe another day, someday.
Say, "one day we'll bring life in Spring." Today
you tell me all the places where you need to go, It's
too much, my soul, it shows/ What if, once we allow
ourselves to breathe, we see our breath freeze when
we plead we belong with rustling autumn leaves while
we're amidst Winter trees, the only sound of
skele-        brittle        branches
break         ache          king,
sleep         soaring        end on
snow, we     fumble to our   numb knees
plead for just one more hour with the sun? The hour only
four, beg for more, more      light. It isn't time for, too
too early for, our night.      The hissing wind births
blizzard, a gust of snow to snap and bend a tree
onto   the bed of silent snow, care-s sed
by   the falling, falling flow  of  soft
soft  snow, frozen with no-  where
to go, vanishing into the sleep
of white, white snow, of white,
white sky, of bright, bright
my un-seeing eye    !!
                     !!!
                    Just
                   Another
                    Dose
                     of
                   Coffee
Give me another dose of this feeling.
I think I'm getting close to achieving. Just
give me another dose. I'll conceal me,   give
me more than what I need to succeed       in
this world of corporate greed. I'll do...more,
I will be alive, a lie. I'll to fly all
the way up, up, up into the sky.
Give me another dose of this feeling. I think I am
coming close to believing in the real me. No
more concealing. Heal me.

Feeling Out

## How Can I

How can I
be a label and me?
How can I
self-identify without a label to identify?
My rhythm is off.

## Hetero/Homo

*Could the times I've been attracted to guys  
negate the times I've gotten lost in your eyes?*

## When The Rhymes Don't Come

*feeling passion with no rhyme  
or rational  
beats not feeling at all.*

*When the English language fails,  
learning another tongue derails.*

## ???????

~~Sexual abuse~~
Is it rape when I say okay,
as I watch my body while my spirit
floats away...?

## Female, Framed

Wear your hells,| Stand up tall, not
bust out that ass. next to him
Wear make-up, but Don't look eye
not too much. Smile to-eye with him.
more, **don't be so** **Keep your virtue,**
cross. Darling, it's cross those legs.
not much to ask. He wants you,
Don't be **so cross.** **uncross those,**
legs, come on,
girl, you know
you're fat, you
are lucky he
wants some of
that. Open Up
share what's there.
Let him take off
your underwear.
Sexy babe can't
go to waste.
I don't care if
you're in pain
darling, why
should he refrain?
He is right, and
you are wrong.
If that's what you
chose to wear,

he can
slip his
hand down
there.

## The Toll

Do not let the words control
the way you think about
your whole,
how you fulfill
your own life's role,
the weight of
words
does take
its
t
o
l
l.

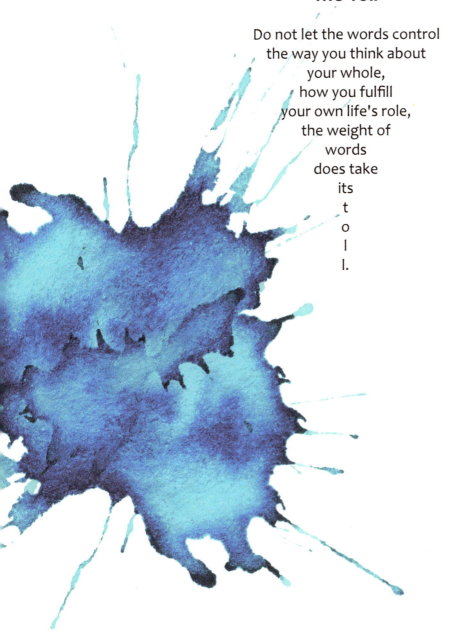

## Her: A Hymn

Let me sing a hymn that I can master.
You won't want to miss it.
Today, I won't make up
my face. No eye-shadow. No blush. Raw lips,
slightly chapped. I'll throw on a tee-shirt and sneakers.
You'll say I'm the one
who wears the pants.
Yesterday, you called me a femme, a lipstick. I made up
my face real sweet. Baby blue
bruise-colored eyelids, a pucker stained like
blood.  Strapped talons on my heels, four inches;
try to knock me down and
I'll stand taller.
Let me sing a her that I can mistress.
You won't want to master it, but in the end, you'll whisper *shhh*he.

## *Shhh*he

I confine myself within
the lines
of letters, smushed into words. I'm open-mouthed
for every vowel, uh— fumbling to
speak my fluidity to fruition.
In defense of my diffidence what's the difference if
I speak or— where're words
for me in the dichotomy of diction?

My given pronoun— she—
sets me like the
sinking sun,
shushing my
"he"
before my day is
done, but
I
am     e
rising,  s
I     i
will   r

I begin to whisper words, to
      speak my sunrise—
you and I, both, stand, mesmerized
by the rainbow of the rising sun.

```
I        E
am       S
rising,  I
I        R
```

My pronoun's they and

    *they* **are** just as singular as you **are.**

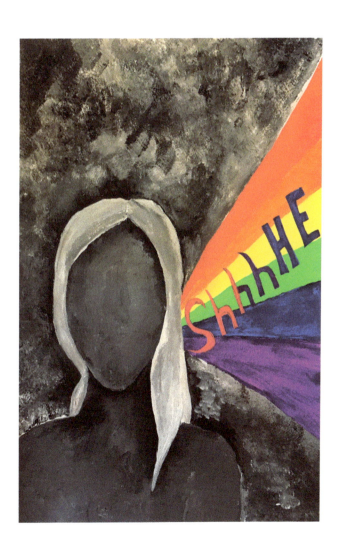

## Shy Girl

I am not that shy girl anymore.
I am not so quiet as before.

*My words can break, my words can make.*
*My words will frustrate,*
*my words will elate.*
*My words will come out dry,*
*but, sometimes, dew-drop sweet.*
*They will wither, they will fly.*

*I'll take*
*whole-hearted*
*responsibility for my hostility, for*
*all the years I've held my soul*
*hostage in my mind*
*to be a pretty, quiet girl, confined.*

If you try to break me,
I will only recreate myself
into a stronger version of myself.
From now on,
I'll make the choice to use my
voice—it's worth fighting for.
Hear me, hear me, **ROAR!**

Feeling Out

My body.
My pleasure.
Mine. My
**POWER**
flowering
blossoms
with.
Baited.
Breath. Let
it out. Toes
tight feels
right
legs
taught
tension
grows


life
itself that
flows

## Inner Piece

a part of me
apart from me

I write to get it right
I write to get it left
behind

by containing
my explaining
into
words,
by constraining
my explaining
in two words
I
love

## Set Your Journey

C.M. Love

Change my last name
and give it up to love.

See 'em love, but
dont forget to
Cary Love

Feeling Out

# About The Artists

Carolyn Fado is a teacher and artist from Washington, DC and Oxford, England. Fado is coming back into the world of writing after a brief hiatus filled with teaching in Bulgaria, Virginia, and Washington, DC. Fado's plays have been performed at the College of Wooster in Ohio ("Memory-Morrow" and "LenOre") and Horizon Theatre in Atlanta ("The Love Pill"). Feeling Out is Fado's first poetry publication.

Carolyn Fado
IG: @cmlovepoet

Kelly Inviere is a poet, author, blogger, and artist living in the greater Washington, D.C. area with her wife and two cats. She is thrilled to be collaborating on this project with Carolyn Fado, combining their shared passion for the written word and visual art to explore the process of coming out in the queer community. Kelly also has a published collection of poems, Where the Light Shines Through: A Memoir in Poetry, in which she tells her story of love, loss, growth and self-discovery.

Kelly Inviere
IG: @kellyinviere
www.kellyinviere.com

Carley Meredith is a artist and graphic designer from Maryland who graduated with her BA in Visual Design from UMBC. Carley's inspiration comes from music, cinema and psychedelic art. Each piece is brought to life through her use of color, contrast and putting her own spin on all she creates with various mediums such as digital, oil, acrylic and leather paint.

Carley Meredith
www.carleymeredith.com

# Artists' Note

When putting together Feeling Out, we collaborated on a lot and worked as a team. Carolyn put it very aptly, stating that it was more akin to creating a stage production than an art book. So, to give credit where credit is due (and to clarify for you, the reader), we wanted to break down the roles we played in this endeavor. Carolyn was our playwright, composing the majority of the poetry and was the mastermind behind the shape poetry images. Kelly was our director, set designer, and production manager. She did the paintings, and organized the original composition of this book, making sure it flowed and that the story unfolded the way we wanted it to. There was overlap with each sharing insight on the other's works, in addition to the co-written piece, POWER (pg. 96).

We were also very lucky to have had the addition of a drawing by the very talented Jean Wogaman for Role Away (pg.77), and the finishing touches that pulled everything together are to the credit of our fantastic graphic designer, Carley Meredith.

Feeling Out

CPSIA information can be obtained
at www.ICGtesting.com
Printed in the USA
BVHW060218051221
623047BV00001B/6